W9-CBQ-708

Pig Out

Pig Out

60 fab recipes for sweet indulgence

MQP

Published by **MQ Publications Limited**
12 The Ivories
6–8 Northampton Street
London N1 2HY
Tel: +44 (0)20 7359 2244
Fax: +44 (0)20 7359 1616
email: mail@mqpublications.com
website: www.mqpublications.com

DESIGN: **Balley Design Associates**
EDITOR: **Leanne Bryan**

ISBN: 1-84072-597-4

10 9 8 7 6 5 4 3 2 1

Printed and bound in France

Introduction

Are you tired of dieting, calorie-counting, and trying to eat your favorite foods in moderation? The constant barrage of healthy eating advice can take all the joy out of eating. It's at times like these that you need to rediscover the pleasure of food.

Prepare yourself for an explosive riot of the senses: Experience the seductive fragrance of a freshly baked Lemon & Lime Love Cake; sample the mouthwatering flavor of Vanilla Poached Pears with butterscotch sauce; behold the vibrant spectacle of a delicious Mandarin Paradise Parfait; relish the crunch of the perfect Double Choc-Chip Cookie; and enjoy the delicate melt-in-the-mouth texture of the truly decadent Chocolate & Chestnut Vacherin.

Searching for a sneaky treat to satisfy the midnight munchies? Delve into The Cookie Jar to beat the craving. Need a comforting pudding for a cold winter evening? Look no further than our Sweet Surrender chapter. Or perhaps you want something for those blue days when nothing but a chocolate fucled pick mc up will do? Go straight to Chocolate Heaven!

Go ahead and indulge yourself—Pig Out!

1

Sweet Surrender

Mouthwatering cakes, tarts,
& puddings

Mississippi Mud Pie

This deliciously rich dessert was among Elvis's favorites, and, appropriately, it originated in the state where he was born—Mississippi.

SERVES 8

6 tbsp butter, at room temperature
1 cup all-purpose flour
2 tbsp iced water
½ cup chopped walnuts
2 cups heavy cream
1 cup confectioners' sugar
1¼lb cream cheese
6oz instant chocolate pudding mix
4 cups milk
1 heaping tsp cocoa powder
Cocoa powder and chopped nuts,
   to decorate

1 Preheat the oven to 350°F.

2 Rub together the butter and flour with your fingertips until the mixture resembles fine bread crumbs. Stir the water and walnuts into the mixture until evenly distributed. Press the mixture into a 9in tart pan.

3 Bake the base 12–15 minutes. Remove from the oven and let cool.

4 Whip the cream to soft peaks. In a separate bowl, combine the confectioners' sugar, cream cheese, and half of the cream, reserving the rest for the topping. Gently spread the mixture over the cooked base and chill in the refrigerator.

5 In a bowl, prepare the chocolate pudding mix using the milk, according to the packet instructions. Mix in the cocoa powder. Spread the chocolate pudding mix over the chilled pie.

6 Decorate with the remaining whipped cream and chopped nuts. Dust with a fine layer of cocoa powder. Refrigerate for a further 4 hours before serving.

Lemon & Lime Love Cake

This tangy loaf is known by lots of different names, but Love Cake is particularly appropriate since everyone who tries it finds it impossible to resist.

MAKES 1 LOAF

6 tbsp butter, at room temperature, plus extra for greasing
1½ cups all-purpose flour, plus extra for dusting
2 tsp baking powder
¼ tsp salt
1¼ cups sugar
2 eggs, lightly beaten
½ cup milk
Grated peel of 1 lemon and juice of ½ lemon
Grated peel and juice of 1 lime

1 Preheat the oven to 325°F. Grease and flour a 9 x 5in loaf pan. Mix together the flour, baking powder, and salt in a large bowl.

2 Put the butter in another bowl and add ¾ cup of the sugar. Beat until pale and creamy, then gradually beat in the eggs, adding a little flour if the mixture shows any sign of curdling. Gradually add the remaining flour, alternating with the milk, beating well after each addition. Stir in the lemon and lime peel.

3 Spoon the mixture into the prepared loaf pan and level the surface. Bake 40–50 minutes, until a skewer inserted into the center of the cake comes out clean. Invert the loaf onto a wire rack, then turn it right way up.

4 Mix the citrus juices with the remaining sugar. Put a tray underneath the rack and spoon the sugar mixture over the top of the loaf, letting it run down the sides slightly. Allow to cool before slicing.

Butterscotch Torte

A truly sumptuous torte that is ideal for special occasions.

SERVES 8

1 cup butter, at room temperature
1 cup sugar
4 eggs, beaten
2 tsp vanilla extract
1¾ cups self-rising flour, sifted
Filling
½ cup butter
Scant 1 cup dark brown sugar
⅓ cup boiling water
1½ cups heavy cream
1 cup milk
3 tbsp cornstarch

1 Preheat the oven to 375°F. Butter and bottom-line three 7in cake pans.

2 Beat the butter with the sugar until light and fluffy. Beat in the eggs, little by little, and fold in the vanilla extract and flour. Spoon into the cake pans and level off the top. Bake 20–25 minutes until firm, springy, and golden. Turn out onto wire racks and let cool.

3 To make the filling, melt the butter in a saucepan and stir in the sugar. Boil for 1 minute, then stir in the water—be careful, it will bubble up. Remove from the heat. Heat ½ cup of the cream with the milk in a separate saucepan until it reaches boiling point.

4 In a large bowl, mix the cornstarch with a little water. Add the hot cream and milk mixture and stir well. Whisk into the melted butter and sugar and cook for 1 minute over a low heat until thick. Set aside to cool completely.

5 Whip the remaining cream to soft peaks. Place one circle of sponge on a serving plate. Spread over a third of the butterscotch filling and cover with a third of the whipped cream. Press a second circle of sponge on top and repeat with the fillings.

6 Top with the final sponge circle and cover with the remaining butterscotch and cream. This cake will not keep for long and is best served on the day of baking.

Tarte Fine aux Pommes

A classic—this delightful tart is simple to make but, nevertheless, looks extremely impressive.

SERVES 4

12oz ready-made puff pastry
2 tart dessert apples
1½ tbsp confectioners' sugar
2 tbsp apricot jelly
Light cream, to serve

1 Preheat the oven to 375°F.

2 Roll out the pastry thinly and cut out a 9in circle. Transfer to a lightly greased baking sheet.

3 Core, halve, and thinly slice the dessert apples lengthwise. Lay the apple slices on the pastry in concentric circles, overlapping slightly and leaving a ½in margin around the edge. Dust generously with the confectioners' sugar.

4 Transfer the baking sheet to the oven and bake 20–25 minutes until the pastry is risen and the apples are tender and golden at the edges.

5 Gently heat the apricot jelly in a small saucepan, then press through a strainer to remove any large pieces. Brush the warm jelly generously over the hot apple tart to glaze. Let cool slightly and serve warm drizzled with cream.

Passion Fruit Cheesecake

The fragrant flavor of the passion fruit raises this delectable cheesecake to superstar status!

SERVES 8–10

5oz graham crackers
6 tbsp butter, melted
9 passion fruits, halved
1¾lb cream cheese
½ cup sugar
½ cup half-and-half cream
4 eggs, beaten
3 egg yolks
2 tsp vanilla extract

1 Preheat the oven to 325°F.

2 Put the crackers in a food processor and process until they are broken into crumbs. Add the melted butter and blend to mix. Press the mixture into the bottom of a 9in springform cake pan and chill 20 minutes until firm. Cover the outside of the pan with a layer of aluminum foil.

3 Place a strainer over a bowl and spoon in the pulp from six of the passion fruits. With the back of a wooden spoon extract as much juice from the seeds as possible.

4 Put the cream cheese, sugar, and cream in the food processor and blend until smooth. Pour in the eggs and egg yolks and blend again until well mixed. Add the vanilla extract and passion fruit juice and briefly blend. Pour the cheesecake mixture into the pan.

5 Place the pan in a shallow dish and pour in sufficient water to come quarter-way up the sides of the pan. Bake 1¼ hours until just firm. (The aluminum foil around the pan will stop the water from leaking into the cheesecake.) Turn off the oven and leave the cheesecake in the oven for an extra 10 minutes.

6 Chill the cheesecake at least 3–4 hours. Once firm, remove the sides of the pan. Spoon the pulp from the remaining passion fruits over the cheesecake just before serving.

Popovers

The ideal popover—also known as Laplanders, Bouncing Babies, and Breakfast Puffs—is a crisp hollow shell which is well risen, golden, and light. To achieve this, the secret is to beat the batter thoroughly in order to develop the gluten, so that the steam formed during baking is held in a large pocket, causing the popovers to rise.

MAKES 12

2 cups all-purpose flour
½ tsp salt
3 eggs
1½ cups milk
1 tbsp butter, melted, plus extra
  for greasing
Jelly and whipped cream, to serve

1 Preheat the oven to 450°F. Grease a twelve-hole popover pan or deep muffin pan.

2 Sift the flour and salt into a large mixing bowl.

3 Beat the eggs with the milk and stir the mixture gradually into the flour to make a smooth batter. Beat the batter thoroughly with an egg beater or whisk. Stir in the melted butter.

4 Divide the batter between the holes of the preheated popover or muffin pan until each well is half full, and place in the oven on a hot baking sheet. Bake 15 minutes, then reduce temperature to 350°F, and cook another 20 minutes. Serve immediately, filled with jam and whipped cream.

Cook's Tip

The temperature of the oven must be just right: if it is too hot, the popovers will brown before popping; if too cold, they will start to rise and then flop. Use a preheated tin with holes 1¼in deep, to give the popovers plenty of height to rise. Ensure the milk and eggs are at room temperature when mixing the batter. Resist the temptation to open the oven door while cooking!

Banana Tarte Tatin

Easy, rich, and utterly delicious, this dessert is at its best served straight away with whipped cream.

SERVES 4–6

4 tbsp butter
5 bananas
½ cup sugar
2 tbsp boiling water
2 pinches of ground cinnamon
9oz ready-made puff pastry
Whipped cream, to serve

1 Preheat the oven to 400°F. Grease a nonstick 9in cake pan.

2 Slice the bananas into ½in rounds. Melt the butter with the sugar in a large skillet. Add the water and stir over a high heat until the sugar has dissolved and the water is a warm caramel color. Add the bananas to the skillet and cook 1–2 minutes. Sprinkle the cinnamon over the bananas, then spoon them into the greased pan.

3 Roll the pastry into a circle, about 1in bigger than the cake pan. Drape it over the bananas and tuck the edges in. Bake 20 minutes until the pastry is puffed and golden. Place a large serving plate over the pan and turn it upside down so the pastry is on the bottom. Remove the cake pan and leave for 5 minutes before serving with whipped cream.

Vanilla Cream Mille Feuille

For a variation, replace the strawberries with your favorite soft fruit.

SERVES 8

12oz ready-made puff pastry
¼ cup confectioners' sugar
Filling
2 cups milk
1 vanilla bean
1 tsp vanilla extract
5 egg yolks
½ cup sugar
1 tbsp all-purpose flour
1 tbsp cornstarch
1 cup heavy cream
4 cups strawberries, thinly sliced

1 Preheat the oven to 400°F. Roll out the pastry to a rectangle 12 x 8½ in. Halve lengthwise and place on a nonstick baking sheet. Sift the confectioners' sugar over one half of the pastry and score into diamond shapes using the tip of a sharp knife. Chill for 30 minutes.

2 Bake the pastry halves until puffed and golden, 15–20 minutes. Let cool, then split the unsugared pastry horizontally, discarding the top. Split the sugared half horizontally, reserving both pieces.

3 For the filling, place the milk, vanilla bean, and vanilla extract into a large saucepan and slowly bring to a boil. Whisk the egg yolks with the sugar, flour, and cornstarch. Add the hot milk and mix well. Remove the vanilla bean and scrape out the seeds, stirring them into the custard. Cook, stirring well, until the custard has thickened, about 4–5 minutes. Cover with plastic wrap to prevent a skin forming and let cool completely.

4 Whip the cream to soft peaks and fold into the cooled custard. Spread half of the custard over the unsugared piece of pastry and cover with half the strawberries. Place the base of the split sugared piece over the fruit and press down gently. Spread the remaining custard over and top with the remaining strawberries. Place the sugared pastry on top.

Soft Berry Bliss

This simple cheesecake is drizzled with a ruby-red raspberry puree.

SERVES 8

4½oz graham crackers
2 tsp sugar
4 tbsp butter, melted
Filling
7oz cream cheese
6 tbsp sour cream
2 tbsp sugar
Grated peel and juice of 1 lemon
1 vanilla bean, split
Topping
1½ cups fresh raspberries
1 tbsp confectioners' sugar, plus extra
    for dusting

1 Place the crackers in a food processor and process until they are broken into fine crumbs. Mix the crumbs with the sugar and melted butter. Press the mixture into the bottom of an 8in springform cake pan. Chill for 30 minutes.

2 Beat together the cream cheese, sour cream, sugar, and lemon peel and juice. Scrape the seeds out of the vanilla bean and stir them into the cheese mixture. Spoon this over the biscuit-crumb base and smooth the top. Let chill at least 2 hours until firm.

3 To make the the topping, press the raspberries through a strainer placed over a bowl. Stir the confectioners' sugar into the juice from the raspberries. Next, carefully remove the cheesecake from the pan, and cut into wedges. Drizzle the topping over each slice. Lightly dust with confectioners' sugar.

White Chocolate Amaretto Cheesecake

Strictly for adults! This Amaretto-laced cheesecake makes a stunning dinner party treat.

SERVES 10–12

4 tbsp melted butter
16–18 graham crackers
3–4 amaretti cookies
½ tsp almond extract
½ tsp ground cinnamon

Filling

12oz good-quality white chocolate, melted
½ cup heavy cream
1½lb cream cheese
⅓ cup sugar
4 eggs
2 tbsp Amaretto or ½ tsp almond extract
½ tsp vanilla extract

Topping

1¾ cups sour cream
4 tbsp sugar
1 tbsp Amaretto or ½ tsp almond extract
White chocolate curls, to decorate (see page 38)

1 Preheat the oven to 350°F. Grease a 9in springform cake pan.

2 Put the crackers and amaretti cookies in a food processor and process until they are broken into fine crumbs. Pour in the melted butter and blend to mix. Add the butter, almond extract, and cinnamon and blend. Press the crumbs into the bottom and up the sides of the pan. Bake in the oven for 5–7 minutes until firm. Remove to a wire rack, then reduce the oven to 300°F.

3 To make the filling, put the chocolate and cream in heatproof bowl set over a saucepan of simmering water. Heat until the chocolate has melted, then remove from the heat. Let cool slightly.

4 Using an electric mixer, beat the cream cheese in a bowl until smooth. Gradually add the sugar, then each egg, beating well after each addition. Slowly beat in the melted chocolate mixture, the Amaretto or almond extract, and the vanilla extract.

5 Pour into the prepared pan and place on a baking sheet. Bake 45–55 minutes until the edge of the cake is firm, but the center is still slightly soft. Remove to a wire rack.

6 Increase the oven temperature to 400°F. To make the topping, whisk together the sour cream, sugar, and Amaretto or almond extract. Spread over the cheesecake. Return to the oven and bake 5–7 minutes. Turn off the oven, but leave the cheesecake in the oven for a further 1 hour.

7 Remove to a wire rack to cool. Run a sharp knife between the crust and the side of the pan to separate the two. Refrigerate, loosely covered, overnight.

8 To serve, unclip and remove the pan ring. Transfer to a serving plate and decorate with white chocolate curls.

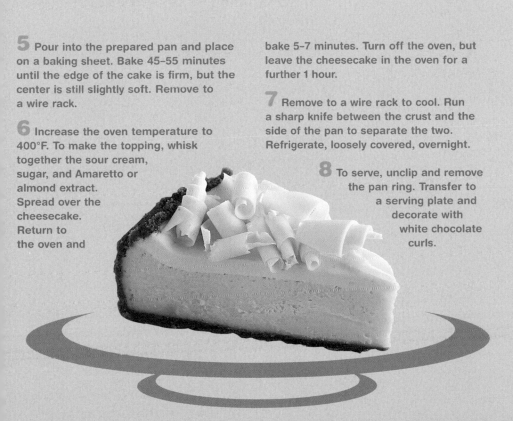

Cappuccino Truffle Cake

This wickedly delicious coffee and chocolate cake is best enjoyed with an espresso at the end of a meal.

SERVES 6–8

1 tbsp instant coffee powder
½ cup hot water
¾ cup ready-to-eat pitted prunes, chopped
4 tbsp Tia Maria or other coffee liqueur
½ cup butter, plus extra for greasing
6oz good-quality semisweet
   chocolate, broken into pieces
5 eggs, separated
½ cup sugar
1 tsp vanilla extract
1 tbsp cornstarch
Cocoa, for dusting
Whipped cream, to serve

1 Dissolve the coffee powder in the hot water, then pour the mixture over the prunes. Add the Tia Maria and let soak overnight.

2 Preheat the oven to 375°F. Grease and line a deep 8in springform cake pan with waxed paper.

3 Heat the chocolate and butter in a heatproof bowl set over a pan of simmering water until melted.

4 Whisk the egg yolks and sugar with a hand-held electric mixer until the mixture becomes thick. Stir in the vanilla extract, prunes and their juice, and the melted chocolate mixture, and set aside.

5 With clean beaters, whisk the egg whites in a nonmetallic bowl until they form stiff peaks. Whisk in the cornstarch and fold into the chocolate mixture. Pour into the prepared pan and bake 50 minutes or until springy to the touch. Let cool in the pan.

6 Cut into slices, dust with cocoa and serve topped with a spoonful of whipped cream.

Georgia Pecan Pie

This well-known pecan dessert is best served with a generous dollop of whipped cream or ice cream.

SERVES 8-10

1½ cups all-purpose flour, plus extra
    for dusting
3oz cream cheese
½ cup butter
2 tbsp sugar
Filling
3–3½ cups pecan halves
3 eggs, lightly beaten
Scant 1 cup firmly packed dark
    brown sugar
½ cup light corn syrup
Grated peel and juice of ½ lemon
4 tbsp butter, melted and cooled
2 tsp vanilla extract
Whipped cream or ice cream, to serve

1 To make the pastry, sift the flour into a large bowl. Add the cream cheese, butter, and sugar and rub with your fingertips until the mixture resembles fine bread crumbs. Form the dough into a ball, then flatten and wrap in plastic wrap. Refrigerate 1 hour.

2 Roll the dough out on a lightly floured surface and carefully line the bottom and sides of a 9in tart pan. Crimp the edge and refrigerate.

3 Preheat the oven to 350°F. Pick out 1 cup perfect pecan halves and set aside. Coarsely chop the remaining nuts.

4 To make the filling, whisk together the eggs and brown sugar until light and foamy. Beat in the syrup, lemon peel and juice, melted butter, and vanilla extract. Stir in the chopped pecans and pour into the tart pan.

5 Set the pie on a baking sheet and carefully arrange the reserved pecan halves in concentric circles on top of the mixture.

6 Bake 45 minutes until the filling has risen and set and the pecans have colored. Transfer to a wire rack to cool to room temperature. Serve with whipped cream or ice cream.

2

Chocolate Heaven
Truly divine chocolate desserts

Chocolate Fudge Cake

This luxurious cake is not for the faint-hearted—the epitome of self-indulgence!

MAKES 8 GENEROUS SLICES

9oz good-quality semisweet
  chocolate, broken into pieces
4 tbsp water
¾ cup butter
¾ cup firmly packed soft brown sugar
4 eggs, beaten
1 cup self-rising flour
¾ cup finely ground almonds

Filling
¾ cup unsweetened cocoa powder
¾ cup firmly packed soft brown sugar
½ cup confectioners' sugar
¾ cup butter, melted
4 tbsp boiling water

Frosting
4oz good-quality semisweet
  chocolate, broken into pieces
4 tbsp butter
1oz sweet chocolate, melted

1 Preheat the oven to 350°F. Melt the chocolate with the water in a heatproof bowl set over a pan of simmering water. Let cool slightly.

2 Beat the butter and sugar together until light and fluffy. Gradually add the beaten eggs. Stir in the melted chocolate, then fold in the flour and ground almonds.

3 Pour the mixture into two greased and lined 8in cake pans and bake in the oven 20–25 minutes. Let cool a little, then invert the cakes onto a wire rack. With a long sharp knife, slice each layer through the center horizontally to make four separate layers.

4 For the filling, mix the cocoa powder, brown sugar, and confectioners' sugar together. Beat in the melted butter and stir in the boiling water to make a smooth paste. Set in the refrigerator for about 20 minutes, then spread evenly over three layers of the cake. Place the final cake layer on top.

5 For the frosting, melt the semisweet chocolate and butter together in a heatproof bowl set over a pan of simmering water. Beat until glossy, then let the mixture cool to a spreading consistency. Smooth evenly over the top of the cake. Drizzle melted sweet chocolate over in a zigzag pattern.

Chocolate Brioche Pudding

This rich, indulgent pudding is surprisingly good eaten cold the day after baking. However, you may not be able to restrain yourself for that long!

SERVES 8

14oz brioche loaf
6 tbsp butter
7oz unsweetened chocolate,
  coarsely chopped
1¼ cups half-and-half cream
1¾ cups packet instant custard
1 cup milk

1 Preheat the oven to 300°F. With a serrated bread knife, remove the crusts from the brioche, then cut into ½in slices. Grease a 9in square gratin dish with a little of the butter, then spread the remaining butter sparingly over the brioche. Lay half the slices in the bottom of the dish.

2 Sprinkle half the chocolate evenly over the brioche, then top with the remaining buttered slices. Bring the cream to a boil in a small saucepan, add the remaining chocolate, and stir until melted.

3 Whisk the custard and milk together, following the packet instructions, and stir in the chocolate cream. Pour the mixture over the brioche and let soak for 30 minutes.

4 Place the gratin dish in a bain-marie (baking pan quarter-filled with water) and bake 55 minutes–1 hour until firm with a little wobble. Let stand 5 minutes before serving.

Kahlua & Chocolate Trifle

This is based on the classic Italian dessert tiramisù, which is traditionally flavored with coffee and laced with liqueur. The Kahlua gives the fresh coffee a bit of a kick.

SERVES 4-6

½ cup strong fresh coffee
4 tbsp Kahlua or other coffee liqueur
6oz ladyfingers
⅓ cup sugar
2 tsp vanilla extract
1lb mascarpone cheese
1 cup heavy cream
4oz unsweetened chocolate, grated
Cocoa powder, to decorate

1 Grease and line a 8½ x 4½ x 2½-in loaf pan with plastic wrap. Mix the coffee and Kahlua together. Dip the ladyfingers into the mixture and use a third of them to line the base of the pan.

2 Whisk the sugar and vanilla extract into the mascarpone with an electric hand-held mixer. Add the cream, a little at a time, whisking on a slow speed until smooth.

3 Spoon half of the mixture on top of the ladyfingers and spread evenly. Add half the grated chocolate, then repeat with a layer of the dipped ladyfingers, the remaining cream mixture, grated chocolate, and a final layer of dipped ladyfingers. Drizzle any remaining coffee mixture over the top.

4 Cover with a layer of plastic wrap, then chill for 2–3 hours. Remove from the pan and peel off the plastic wrap. Dust with a generous amount of cocoa powder, slice, and serve.

Chocolate Profiteroles

A luxurious alternative to the classic profiterole, these miniature cream puffs are filled with chocolate cream.

MAKES 12

1 cup all-purpose flour
1 tbsp confectioners' sugar
Generous ¾ cup water
⅓ cup butter, diced
3 eggs, beaten
1¼ cups heavy cream
2 tbsp drinking chocolate powder
Sauce
4oz good-quality semisweet
  chocolate, broken into pieces
2 tbsp light corn syrup
2 tbsp butter
4 tbsp water

1 Preheat the oven to 400°F. Sift the flour and confectioners' sugar into a small bowl. Place the water and butter in a saucepan and heat gently until the butter has melted. Bring to a boil, then remove from the heat and quickly add the flour mixture, beating until smooth. Transfer to a bowl and let cool.

2 With a hand-held electric mixer, gradually beat the eggs into the mixture to make cream puff paste. Fit a pastry bag with a plain tip and fill with the paste. Pipe twelve rounds onto a nonstick baking sheet. Bake until puffed and golden, 18–20 minutes. Make a hole in the base of each profiterole and let cool on a wire rack.

3 Whip the cream with the chocolate powder until stiff. Fill a new pastry bag with the chocolate cream and pipe carefully into the hole in the base of each individual profiterole.

4 To make the sauce, put the chocolate, syrup, butter, and water into a bowl and place over a pan of gently simmering water. Melt the chocolate and stir to mix. To serve, drizzle the warm chocolate sauce over the profiteroles.

Chocolate & Orange Mousse

Chocolate and orange are perfect partners and this delicious, rich mousse is no exception.

SERVES 4

8oz good-quality semisweet
  chocolate, broken into pieces
Grated peel and juice of 1 large orange
1 tbsp Grand Marnier
4 eggs, separated
½ cup confectioners' sugar
⅔ cup heavy cream
Pared strips of orange peel, to decorate

1 Place the chocolate in a heatproof bowl. Add the orange peel and juice and the Grand Marnier and set over a pan of simmering water. Heat until the chocolate has melted, stir, then let cool.

2 Whisk the egg yolks with the confectioners' sugar until the mixture becomes pale and frothy. Stir into the cooled chocolate mixture.

3 Lightly whip the cream and fold into the mousse mixture. Whisk the egg whites to soft peaks and carefully fold into the mixture. Pour into custard cups, individual ramekins, a soufflé dish, or a glass bowl and chill 3–4 hours until set. Decorate with the orange peel.

White Chocolate Tiramisù

This variation on the classic tiramisù is very, very rich and totally addictive!

SERVES 8–10

8oz good-quality white chocolate,
   broken into pieces
½ cup milk
3 eggs, separated
Scant ½ cup sugar
2lb mascarpone cheese
½ cup marsala wine
8oz amaretti cookies
White chocolate curls
4oz good-quality white chocolate

1 Put the chocolate and milk in a heatproof bowl set over a saucepan of simmering water. Heat until the chocolate has melted, then remove from the heat, stir until smooth, and let cool.

2 Place the egg yolks in a bowl with the sugar and whisk until light and frothy. Beat in the cooled chocolate mixture.

3 Spoon the mascarpone into a large mixing bowl and carefully beat in the chocolate mixture. Don't overwork the mascarpone or it will separate.

4 Beat the egg whites to soft peaks and fold into the mascarpone mixture. Spoon half of the mixture into a serving dish.

5 Pour the marsala wine into a shallow bowl and dip both sides of the amaretti cookies in for about 10 seconds, then arrange on top of the mascarpone mixture. Spoon the remaining mascarpone mixture over and chill for at least 3–4 hours.

6 To make the white chocolate curls, melt the chocolate as in step 1, then spread very thinly over a marble slab or work surface. Let cool until just hard, then draw the blade of a small sharp knife across the surface, keeping it at a slight angle—the chocolate should roll into curls. Place on waxed paper in the refrigerator to set hard, then arrange over the top of the tiramisù to decorate.

Chocolate Marquise
with vanilla crème anglaise

A marquise is a super-rich firm chocolate mousse—delicious!

SERVES 6-8

11oz unsweetened chocolate, broken
  into pieces
¼ cup very strong coffee
½ cup butter
½ cup sugar
4 egg yolks
1⅔ cups heavy cream
Vanilla crème anglaise
1¼ cups milk
1 vanilla bean, split
4 egg yolks
½ cup sugar

1 Line a 8½ x 4½ x 2½-in loaf pan or terrine dish with plastic wrap. Put the chocolate and coffee in a heatproof bowl set over a pan of simmering water. Heat until the chocolate has melted. Stir, then let cool.

2 Beat the butter with ⅓ cup of the sugar until pale and fluffy. In a separate bowl, whisk the egg yolks with the remaining sugar until thickened and pale. Lightly whip the cream until it just begins to hold its shape.

3 Beat the melted chocolate into the butter and fold in the egg yolk mixture, followed by the cream. Pour into the loaf pan and chill 5–6 hours.

4 For the crème anglaise, bring the milk to a boil with the vanilla bean. Beat the egg yolks and sugar together. Add the hot milk, then return the mixture to the pan and stir over low heat until it starts to thicken. Let cool, then scrape out the seeds from the vanilla bean and stir into the cold custard. Chill until ready to serve.

5 To serve, turn the mousse out onto a serving plate and serve with the vanilla crème anglaise.

Chocolate & Strawberry Pavlova

This famous meringue dessert is topped with a mouthwatering chocolate cream and fresh strawberries.

SERVES 8

4 egg whites
Pinch of salt
1 cup sugar
1 tbsp cornstarch
2oz good-quality semisweet
  chocolate, broken into pieces
Pinch of ground cinnamon
Filling
1¼ cups heavy cream
2oz sweet chocolate, cut into
  small pieces
2 tbsp milk
2 cups strawberries, hulled and halved

1 Preheat the oven to 225°F.

2 Whisk the egg whites with the salt until the mixture is stiff. Gradually whisk in the sugar and beat until glossy and thick. Fold in the cornstarch, chocolate pieces, and ground cinnamon.

3 Draw a 7in circle on a piece of waxed paper and place ink-side down on a baking sheet. Spoon the meringue mixture into the center and spread to the circle perimeter, hollowing out the middle slightly. Cook 1–1½ hours. Let cool, then place on a serving plate.

4 To make the filling, whip the cream lightly. Put the sweet chocolate and the milk in a heatproof bowl set over a saucepan of simmering water. Heat until the chocolate has melted, then remove from the heat and let cool slightly. Roughly fold the chocolate mixture into the cream, leaving it a little streaky. Pile the cream into the center of the meringue and arrange the strawberries on top.

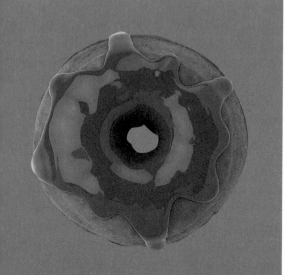

Chocolate-Covered Doughnuts

These delightful doughnuts are a favorite with children, but watch out—they're so good you might not be willing to share!

MAKES 8

2 cups all-purpose flour
¼oz rapid-rise dried yeast
Pinch of salt
¼ cup sugar
2 tbsp butter
⅔ cup milk
2 egg yolks
Oil, for deep frying

Topping
2oz sweet chocolate, broken into pieces

1 Mix the flour in a bowl with the yeast and salt. Add the sugar, then rub in the butter until the mixture resembles fine bread crumbs.

2 Heat the milk in a saucepan until it is warm, then whisk in the egg yolks. Add the liquid to the flour mixture and mix to a soft dough. Cover with plastic wrap and leave in a warm place to prove until the dough has doubled in bulk, about 1 hour.

3 Knock back the dough and knead on a well-floured surface, 5–10 minutes. Roll out the dough until ½in thick, and stamp out rounds with a plain pastry cutter. Make a hole in the middle of each round with your finger. Place the doughnuts on a greased baking sheet and let rise until doubled in size, 40 minutes–1 hour.

4 Deep-fry the doughnuts one at a time in the hot oil heated to 375°F until they are golden brown, about 5 minutes. Drain on paper towels and let cool.

5 Put the sweet chocolate in a heatproof bowl set over a saucepan of simmering water. Heat until it has melted, then remove from the heat. Let cool slightly. Dip the rounded tops of the doughnuts in the melted chocolate and allow to set.

Chocolate Crêpes

with caramelized bananas

Crêpes are a real favorite and can be filled with all manner of sweet and savory goodies, although you can't beat the combination of bananas and cream.

MAKES 10

1¼ cups all-purpose flour
2 tbsp unsweetened cocoa powder
2 tbsp sugar
2 eggs, beaten
1 cup milk
6 tbsp water
1 tbsp oil, plus extra for frying
Filling
4 bananas, sliced
½ cup confectioners' sugar
1¼ cups heavy cream, whipped

1 Mix together the flour, cocoa powder, and sugar in a large bowl. Add the beaten eggs and slowly pour in the milk and water, beating until a smooth batter. Stir in the oil, then let rest about 30 minutes.

2 Brush a large crêpe skillet with a little oil and place over medium heat. Pour in a ladleful of batter and cook until set. Flip the crêpe over and quickly cook the other side. Set aside and keep warm. Repeat with the remaining batter.

3 For the filling, place the sliced bananas on a nonstick baking sheet. Sprinkle with the confectioners' sugar, and cook under a preheated broiler 3–4 minutes until golden. Fill each crêpe with a few banana slices, topped with a spoonful of whipped cream. Fold the crêpes in half or fourths and serve immediately.

Chocolate & Chestnut Vacherin

This impressive layered meringue dessert has a wonderfully rich and creamy chestnut and chocolate filling.

SERVES 8-10

5 egg whites
1¼ cups sugar
2 tsp vanilla extract
1⅔ cups heavy cream
11oz unsweetened chocolate, broken into pieces
8oz unsweetened chestnut puree
3 tbsp brandy
1 cup confectioners' sugar, sifted
1 tbsp cocoa powder, sifted, to decorate

1 Preheat the oven to 250°F. Line three baking sheets with waxed paper. Draw a circle around the base of an 8in/20cm cake pan on each piece of paper.

2 Whisk the egg whites until they form stiff peaks. Beat in the sugar a tablespoon at a time—the mixture should be stiff and glossy. Fold in the vanilla extract.

3 Spoon equal quantities of meringue mixture into the middle of each circle and spread out evenly to the edges. Bake 2 hours, then peel off the paper and let cool on wire racks.

4 Heat the cream in a saucepan until almost boiling. Take off the heat and add the chocolate, stirring until it has melted. Let cool, then chill until the mixture starts to thicken, about 45 minutes. Using an electric whisk, beat the chocolate mixture for 2–3 minutes until light and airy.

5 Mix the chestnut puree with the brandy and confectioners' sugar. Spread half of the chocolate cream over the base of one meringue disc, then spread half of the chestnut mixture over the chocolate. Place a second meringue disc on top and repeat with the remaining chocolate and chestnut mixture. Top with the remaining meringue and dust with cocoa powder.

Forbidden Fruit

Devilishly tempting fresh
fruit desserts

Figgy Meringue Tarts

These tasty little treasures look like simple meringue tarts, but just one bite will reveal a fruity, figgy surprise!

MAKES 4

2 egg whites
½ cup sugar
4 individual deep custard tarts
4 ripe figs

1 Preheat the oven to 425°F. Whisk the egg whites in a large bowl until stiff. Gradually whisk in the sugar a little at a time, whisking well between each addition until the mixture is thick and glossy.

2 Arrange the custard tarts on a baking sheet and bake 6–8 minutes until warmed through. Remove from the oven and top each with a fig.

3 Spoon the meringue mixture evenly over each fig to cover them completely. Using the tip of a knife to gently pull the meringue into peaks. Bake 4–5 minutes until lightly golden and just warm.

Red Currant Swirl

The contrast between the deep red of the currants and the white whirls of sour cream makes this an attractive dessert.

SERVES 4–6

1 cup sugar
2½ cups water
⅔ cup rosé or red wine
5 cups red currants, stripped from
  their stalks
3 tbsp arrowroot mixed to a paste with
  3 tbsp water
4–6 tbsp sour cream

1 Put the sugar in a saucepan with the water. Heat, stirring, until the sugar dissolves, then bring to a boil and cook, without stirring, 2–3 minutes. Stir in the wine.

2 Add the red currants to the wine syrup, lower the heat, and poach them for about 10 minutes until just tender.

3 Stir in the arrowroot paste. Bring to a boil, stirring all the time until the mixture thickens. Let cool, then chill for several hours. Serve in individual glass dishes, swirling 1 tbsp of sour cream on the surface of each portion.

Cook's Tip

Arrowroot is preferable to cornstarch for thickening this particular sauce as it gives a clear, rather than a cloudy, result.

Lychees
with orange & ginger

A refreshing, simple dessert that looks as good as it tastes.

SERVES 4

½ cup sugar
1¼ cups water
2 oranges
16 lychees, peeled and pitted
2 pieces drained preserved ginger, sliced
2 passion fruits, halved

1 Heat the sugar and water in a small saucepan, stirring until the sugar has dissolved, then boil the syrup for 1 minute without stirring.

2 Pour the syrup into a serving bowl and let stand until cold. Peel and segment the oranges, working over the bowl of syrup so that any juice is incorporated. Add the orange segments to the bowl, together with the lychees and ginger. Stir lightly to combine the ingredients.

3 Divide between individual glass dishes. Spoon the passion fruit pulp over the top and serve at once.

Lemon Meringue Pie

This frothy 1950s confection is full of tangy flavor and rich textures. For alternative toppings, sprinkle with flaked coconut, sliced almonds, or miniature marshmallows before baking.

SERVES 8

9in baked pie shell
Filling
1 cup sugar
¼ cup cornstarch
1 cup boiling water
3 egg yolks, lightly beaten
2 tbsp butter
Finely grated peel and juice of
  1 large lemon
Meringue
3 egg whites, at room temperature
¼ tsp cream of tartar
6 tbsp sugar
½ tsp vanilla extract

1 Preheat the oven to 450°F.

2 For the filling, combine the sugar and cornstarch over low heat and slowly add the boiling water, stirring constantly. Bring to a boil, then simmer until the mixture becomes transparent and thickens, still stirring, about 5 minutes.

3 Place the lightly beaten egg yolks in a separate bowl. Remove the sugar and cornstarch mixture from the heat and gradually pour the hot liquid into the yolks. Set the bowl over a pan of simmering water. Stir in the butter, lemon juice and peel and continue to cook until the filling becomes very thick. Let cool, then pour into the prepared pie shell.

4 To make the meringue, whisk the egg whites until frothy. Add the cream of tartar and continue whisking. Drizzle in the sugar and vanilla extract and continue whisking until they form stiff peaks. Take care not to overwhisk.

5 Pile the meringue onto the lemon filling, swirling lightly from the center towards the edges, ensuring that it touches the pastry all around. Use the tip of a knife to gently pull the meringue into peaks. Bake in the center of the oven until the meringue is a delicate brown, 10–15 minutes.

Apple & Calvados Soufflé

This fantastic soufflé combines tart apples with sweet Calvados. Individual soufflé dishes look the most impressive but a large one could also be used.

SERVES 4

3 tbsp butter, plus extra for greasing
1 tbsp graham cracker crumbs
⅓ cup all-purpose flour
¾ cup milk
3 tbsp Calvados or other apple brandy
2 tart dessert apples, peeled, cored, and sliced
2 tsp grated lemon peel
2 tbsp fresh lemon juice
½ cup sugar
4 eggs, separated
Confectioners' sugar, for dusting

1 Preheat the oven to 375°F. Grease six 1½ cup soufflé dishes or one 8 cup soufflé dish and scatter the graham cracker crumbs around the sides and over the base.

2 Melt the remaining butter in a saucepan and add the flour. Remove from the heat and gradually stir in the milk. Return the pan to the heat and bring to a boil, whisking gently until the mixture thickens. Cook for 1 minute, then remove from the heat and whisk in the Calvados. Cover the sauce and set aside to cool.

3 In a covered pan, cook the apples with the lemon peel and juice and 1 tbsp of the sugar, stirring occasionally, until softened, 5–6 minutes. Puree and let cool slightly. Meanwhile, whisk the egg yolks into the cooled sauce, then stir in the apple puree.

4 Whisk the egg whites until stiff. Gradually whisk in the remaining sugar until the mixture is glossy. Stir a spoonful of the whites into the sauce, then fold in the rest. Spoon the mixture into the individual soufflé dishes or large soufflé dish. Wipe the top of the dishes, and bake 20–35 minutes, depending on dish size. Resist the temptation to open the oven door while cooking. Dust the top with confectioners' sugar before serving.

Luxury Black Currant Pudding

Fresh black currants add a refreshing tang to this luxurious bread and butter pudding. Let the pudding stand to cool for a while before eating, or, even better, serve cold with extra cream.

SERVES 4

4 tbsp butter, at room temperature
8 medium–thick slices of bread
2 cups fresh or frozen black currants
5 eggs
⅓ cup sugar
2½ cups whole milk, or half-and-half cream
2 tsp vanilla extract
Freshly grated nutmeg
1 tbsp light brown sugar, to scatter
Lightly whipped cream, to serve

1 Preheat the oven to 350°F. Butter a 2-quart baking dish.

2 Remove the crusts from the bread and discard. Spread the slices with the butter, then cut diagonally in half. Layer the bread slices in the dish, buttered-side up, scattering the black currants between the layers as you go.

3 Whisk the eggs and sugar together lightly in a mixing bowl, then gradually whisk in the milk or cream, vanilla extract, and a pinch of nutmeg.

4 Pour the mixture over the bread, pushing the slices down well to soak them thoroughly. Scatter with the light brown sugar and some more nutmeg. Place the dish in a baking pan a quarter filled with hot water. Bake 1 hour until the top is crisp and golden. Let cool slightly, then serve with lightly whipped cream.

Pan-fried Panettone
with nectarines

Panettone makes marvelous French toast, but if you can't find it, use brioche or any fruity bread instead.

SERVES 4

2 eggs, beaten
2 tbsp sugar
½ cup milk
½ cup half-and-half cream
¼ tsp vanilla extract
4 tbsp butter
2 nectarines, pitted and sliced
2 tbsp light brown sugar
4 slices panettone (or 2 large slices, halved diagonally)

1 Put the eggs in a shallow bowl large enough to hold one of the slices of panettone. Stir in the sugar, then the milk, cream, and vanilla extract.

2 Melt half the butter in a large skillet, add the nectarines, and sprinkle them with the light brown sugar. Cook the nectarines, shaking the skillet frequently, until soft and caramelized. Spoon into a dish and keep hot.

3 Melt the remaining butter in the skillet. Dip a slice of panettone into the egg mixture, turning it to coat it on both sides. Transfer the panettone into the skillet and cook it over medium heat, about 2 minutes, then turn it over carefully, as it is quite delicate, and cook the other side for 2 minutes.

4 Prepare the second slice of panettone in the same way, adding more butter to the skillet if necessary and keeping the cooked panettone hot. (If your skillet is large enough, cook two slices at once.) Serve the panettone with the nectarines.

Summer Berry Shortcake

These delectable fruit-filled shortcakes are the perfect mid-afternoon treat for a lazy summer day.

MAKES 8 SHORTCAKES

6 cups strawberries, hulled and
 sliced, or a mixture of strawberries,
 raspberries, blueberries, and blackberries
2–3 tbsp sugar
1–2 tbsp raspberry juice or 1 tbsp
 orange juice
1 cup heavy cream, whipped to soft
 peaks and chilled
A few berries, confectioners' sugar, and
 mint leaves, to decorate
Shortcake
2 cups all-purpose flour, plus extra
 for dusting
2½ tsp baking powder
½ tsp salt
2 tbsp sugar, plus extra for sprinkling
6 tbsp butter, diced
1 cup heavy cream

1 Preheat the oven to 425°F.

2 Put the berries in a bowl and toss in the sugar and fruit juice. Let stand until the juices begin to run, stirring occasionally.

3 To make the shortcake, mix together the flour, baking powder, salt, and sugar in a large bowl. Add the butter and rub in using a pastry blender or fingertips until the mixture resembles coarse bread crumbs. Whip the cream and, using a fork, lightly stir in all but 1 tbsp of it, little by little, until a soft dough is formed.

4 Turn out onto a lightly floured work surface and knead the dough 6–8 times. Pat or roll it into a rectangle about ½in thick. Using a round cutter, stamp out eight rounds or, if you prefer, cut into eight 3in squares. Arrange 3in apart on a baking sheet. Brush the tops with the remaining cream, and sprinkle with sugar.

5 Bake until set and the tops are pale golden, about 10 minutes. Transfer the shortcakes to a wire rack to cool.

6 Using a fork or serrated knife, split each shortcake horizontally. Place the bottoms on dessert plates, and spoon the berry mixture equally over each. Spoon the chilled whipped cream over the berries. Top with the other half of shortcake and decorate each with a sliced berry, confectioners' sugar and a mint leaf.

Vanilla Poached Pears
with butterscotch sauce

**A simple yet elegant and delicious fruit
dessert. Mouthwatering when served
with vanilla ice cream or whipped cream.**

SERVES 6

6 ripe pears, peeled
3–4 cups water
¾ cup sugar
2 vanilla beans, split lengthwise
Pared peel of ½ lemon
Vanilla ice cream or whipped cream, to
  serve (optional)
Sauce
4 tbsp butter
⅓ cup light brown sugar
½ cup light corn syrup
½ cup heavy cream

1 Stand the pears in a saucepan just big
enough for them to fit snugly. Pour enough
water over to just cover and add the sugar,
vanilla beans, and lemon peel.

2 Bring to a boil, then reduce the heat
and simmer 40–50 minutes until the pears
are softened but still hold their shape. (If
the pears aren't very ripe this might take a
bit longer.) Remove from the heat and let
the pears cool in the syrup.

3 To make the butterscotch sauce, melt
the butter with the light brown sugar
and syrup. Stir in ½ cup of the cooled
pear syrup and simmer 2–3 minutes.
Stir in the cream and simmer for a further
2–3 minutes.

4 Remove the pears to a serving dish
and either pour a little butterscotch sauce
over each pear, or serve it separately in a
jug. Serve with vanilla ice cream or
whipped cream, if desired.

Strawberries Romanoff

When strawberries are at their peak, their intense flavor requires little, if any, adornment. However, strawberries which have been in cold storage sometimes need a helping hand, and this is a very good way to serve them.

SERVES 4–6

6 sugar lumps
1 orange
6 tbsp Grand Marnier
6 cups strawberries, hulled
Crème chantilly
1¼ cups heavy cream
1 tbsp confectioners' sugar
½ tsp vanilla extract

1 Rub the sugar lumps over the surface of the orange to impregnate them with the fruit's oils. Put the lumps in a bowl. Halve the orange, then squeeze it and strain the juice into the bowl. Crush the sugar lumps in the juice, then stir in the Grand Marnier.

Add the strawberries, stir, then cover and chill for 2 hours. Stir occasionally, taking care not to break up the fruit.

2 To make the crème chantilly, whip the cream until it forms soft peaks, then stir in the confectioners' sugar and vanilla extract. Spoon the mixture into a piping bag fitted with a star nozzle.

3 Drain the strawberries. Pile them up, pyramid fashion, on a serving dish, preferably one with a stand, and decorate by piping the cream into the gaps and around the pyramid.

Variation

For sheer indulgence, make small meringues, roughly the same size as the strawberries, and add them to the pyramid with the cream.

Pineapple Upside-Down Cake

A cake much loved for its spectacular appearance. Another Elvis favorite— he adored the ginger-peach version.

SERVES 8

4 tbsp butter
Scant ½ cup light brown sugar
15oz can pineapple rings in natural
  juice, drained, reserving 5 tbsp juice
7 red candied cherries
2 tbsp whole pecans (optional)
1 cup self-rising flour, sifted
1 tsp baking powder
Pinch of salt
1 cup sugar
3 eggs, separated
½ tsp vanilla extract
¼ tsp almond extract
Evaporated milk or light cream, to serve

1 Preheat the oven to 350°F.

2 Reserve 1 tbsp of the butter, then melt the rest over low heat. Pour into a 9in springform cake pan and sprinkle the light brown sugar evenly over it. Arrange the pineapple rings in the butter-sugar mixture, placing a cherry in the center of each ring. Fill in the spaces with pecans, if desired.

3 In a separate bowl, sift the flour, baking powder, and salt together. In another bowl, cream the reserved 1 tbsp of butter with the sugar.

4 Beat the egg yolks until pale and slowly fold into the creamed mixture, continuing to beat until fluffy. Add the reserved pineapple juice, vanilla and almond extracts, and the flour. Whisk the egg whites until they form stiff peaks and fold into the mixture.

5 Pour the mixture over the pineapple. Bake 30–35 minutes. Let cool in the pan on a wire rack. Loosen the cake with a spatula, cover with a serving plate and invert, so that the pineapple and cherry base with its runny, butterscotch topping is now on top. Remove the pan. Serve warm with evaporated milk or light cream.

Variations

Use apricots, peach, or pear halves—either stewed, canned, or fresh—instead of pineapple. To try Elvis's favorite, use peaches instead of pineapples and add ½ tsp ground cinnamon and 2 tsp ground dried ginger to the butter-sugar mixture. Another winning combination is 2 tbsp flaked coconut instead of pecans.

Cherry Syllabub

The joy of this dessert is that any flavored liqueur or spirit of your choice can be added to the basic mixture. Also the fruit can be varied depending on the season and your preference.

SERVES 4

½ cup sweet white wine
4 tbsp white or coconut rum
2 tbsp fresh lemon juice
Scant ½ cup sugar
1¾ cups heavy cream
11 oz fresh pitted cherries
Crisp almond cookies, to serve

1 In a large bowl combine the white wine, rum, lemon juice, and sugar, and mix well until the sugar has dissolved.

2 Stir in the cream and then whip until stiff enough to hold soft peaks. Spoon the cherries into the bases of four glasses and top with the cream syllabub.

3 Serve immediately with crisp almond cookies to dip into the cream. If left to stand for too long the mixture will separate out again.

Seared Fruit
in frothy orange sauce

This out-of-the-ordinary gratin is strictly for adults! A colorful combination of fruits are immersed in a frothy egg-based sauce flavored with orange liqueur.

SERVES 4

2 fresh figs, cut into wedges
½ pineapple, peeled, cored, and cut into chunks
1 ripe mango, peeled, pitted, and cut into chunks
1½ cups blackberries
4 tbsp white wine
⅓ cup sugar
6 egg yolks
2 tbsp Cointreau or other orange liqueur

1 Divide the prepared fruit between four individual gratin dishes and scatter the blackberries over the top.

2 Heat the wine and sugar in a saucepan over medium heat until the sugar has dissolved. Cook 5 minutes.

3 Put the egg yolks in a large heatproof bowl. Set the bowl over a pan of simmering water and whisk the yolks until they have thickened and are pale and fluffy. Slowly pour the syrup into the egg yolks, with the Cointreau, whisking continuously until thickened.

4 Spoon the frothy mixture over the fruit and place under a hot broiler on a low shelf and broil until the topping is golden. Serve immediately.

New England Blueberry Pancakes

These delightful pancakes are a great breakfast treat and are a delicious accompaniment to fried eggs, crispy bacon, or sausages.

SERVES 4-6

1¼ cups all-purpose flour
½ tsp baking powder
½ tsp baking soda
¼ tsp salt
1 cup buttermilk
¾ cup milk
1 tbsp sugar or honey
2 tbsp butter, melted
½ tsp vanilla extract
½ cup fresh blueberries
Vegetable oil, for frying
Butter and maple syrup or honey, to serve

1 In a bowl, combine the flour, baking powder, baking soda, and salt, and make a well in the center.

2 In another bowl, whisk together the buttermilk, about ½ cup of the milk, the sugar or honey, melted butter, and vanilla extract. Pour the liquid mixture into the well and stir gently until just combined; if the batter is too thick, add a little more milk, as it should be pourable. Do not overbeat—a few floury lumps may remain. Gently fold in the blueberries.

3 Heat a large skillet or nonstick pancake griddle over medium heat, and brush with the vegetable oil. Drop the batter in small ladlefuls into the skillet and cook until the edges are set and the surface beings to bubble, about 1 minute.

4 Turn each pancake and cook until the bottoms are just golden, about 30 seconds. Transfer to a baking sheet and keep warm in an oven on low heat. Continue with the remaining batter. Serve hot with butter and maple syrup or honey.

The Cookie Jar

Irresistible brownies, muffins, & cookies

Chocolate Chunk Brownies

No one knows the origin of the first batch of brownies, but the popularity of this American standard never wanes!

MAKES 12 BROWNIES

¾ cup butter
4oz good-quality semisweet
  chocolate, broken into pieces
1¾ cups sugar
3 eggs
1¾ cups all-purpose flour
1½ tsp vanilla extract
½ tsp salt
6oz sweet chocolate, broken
  into pieces
½ cup chopped pecans or walnuts
Ice cream or whipped cream, to serve

1 Preheat the oven to 350°F. Lightly grease a 13 x 9in nonstick baking pan. In a saucepan, melt the butter and semisweet chocolate over low heat, stirring frequently. Remove from the heat and stir in the sugar until it is dissolved. Set aside to cool slightly.

2 Add the eggs one at a time, beating well after each addition. Stir in the flour, vanilla extract, and salt until just blended, then fold in the sweet chocolate and nuts. Do not overmix. Evenly spread the mixture in the pan, pushing into the corners.

3 Bake until set: the top will be shiny and a skewer inserted into the center will come out with a few wet crumbs still attached, 25–30 minutes. Do not overbake. Transfer to a wire rack to cool completely, then cut into squares. Serve with ice cream or whipped cream.

Blueberry Muffins

In 1956 Fats Domino found his thrill on Blueberry Hill. Find yours with these moist, tasty muffins crammed with succulent fruit!

MAKES 12

1¾ cups all-purpose flour, sifted
½ cup sugar
1 tbsp baking powder
½ tsp salt
1 cup blueberries, huckleberries, or bilberries
1 egg
½ cup milk
4 tbsp butter, melted

1 Preheat the oven to 425°F. Place twelve paper muffin cases in a muffin tin.

2 Sift the dry ingredients together into a large bowl. Gently distribute the berries. In a different bowl, beat the egg, then pour in the milk and melted butter.

3 Combine the wet and dry ingredients and stir briskly until the flour is moistened—the mixture should appear rough and lumpy. Fill the paper muffin cups about two-thirds full. Bake 20–25 minutes until risen, and serve while still warm.

Variations

Half a cup of any of the following dried fruits (or a combination) can be added to the dry ingredients, chopped, sliced, or whole: apricots, dates, currants, figs, peaches, prunes. Chopped walnuts and dates make a particularly good combination.

Coffee & Cinnamon Cookies

These sophisticated crescent-shaped cookies are a delicious accompaniment to a relaxing morning coffee.

MAKES ABOUT 40

1 cup butter, plus extra for greasing
1 tbsp instant coffee granules
1 tbsp boiling water
¾ cup sugar
1 tbsp Kahlua or other coffee liqueur
3½ cups all-purpose flour
2 tsp ground cinnamon
¼ cup confectioners' sugar

1 Preheat the oven to 350°F. Lightly grease two baking sheets.

2 Dissolve the coffee in the water. Beat the butter and sugar together until pale and fluffy. Beat in the coffee and liqueur. Sift the flour and 1 tsp of the cinnamon together, then beat into the mixture.

3 Take small amounts of the mixture, each about the size of a walnut, and roll into balls. Shape each ball first into a log, then curve into a crescent. Space well apart on the baking sheets. Bake 12 minutes or until golden. Let cool on the baking sheets, 2–3 minutes, then transfer to a wire rack to cool completely.

4 Sift the confectioners' sugar and remaining cinnamon together a couple of times to ensure that the sugar and spice are well mixed. Dust the cookies with the spiced sugar. Cookies can be stored in an airtight container up to five days.

Chocolate Hazelnut & Vanilla Whirls

These attractive and flavorsome little cookies are surprisingly simple to make.

MAKES ABOUT 30

¾ cup butter, plus extra for greasing
¾ cup confectioners' sugar
1 tsp vanilla extract
2 cups all-purpose flour, sifted, plus extra for dusting
2 tbsp chocolate and hazelnut spread
1 tbsp unsweetened cocoa powder, sifted

1 Preheat the oven to 325°F. Lightly grease a baking sheet.

2 Beat together the butter and sugar until pale and fluffy. Beat in the vanilla extract. Add the flour and work into the mixture to form a soft dough. Divide the dough into two pieces and work the chocolate and hazelnut spread and cocoa powder into one half.

3 Roll each piece of dough on a lightly floured surface to form two rectangles about 6 x 8in. Place one piece of dough on top of the other and press together lightly. Trim the edges and roll up lengthwise like a jelly roll. Cover and chill 30 minutes.

4 Cut the dough into ¼in slices and space well apart on the baking sheet. Bake 10–12 minutes until crisp. Let cool 2–3 minutes on the baking sheet, then transfer to a wire rack to cool completely. Cookies can be stored in an airtight container up to 1 week.

Cook's Tip

The dough should be quite soft. You may find it easier to handle if you roll it out on waxed paper. If it is too soft to roll, chill 10–15 minutes to firm slightly.

Chocolate Chip Muffins

These muffins are even naughtier when served drizzled with melted chocolate!

MAKES 15

3 cups self-rising flour
Pinch of salt
6 tbsp sugar
⅔ cup good-quality semisweet
    chocolate chips
4 tbsp butter
6oz good-quality semisweet
    chocolate, broken into pieces
2 eggs, beaten
1¼ cups buttermilk
½ cup milk

1 Preheat the oven to 425°F. Place fifteen paper muffin cases into a muffin pan.

2 Mix together the flour, salt, sugar, and chocolate chips in a large bowl.

3 Melt the butter and chocolate together in a bowl set over a pan of simmering water, then let cool. Whisk in the eggs, buttermilk, and milk.

4 Combine the wet and dry ingredients and stir briskly until the flour is moistened. The mixture should appear rough and lumpy. Fill the paper muffin cases about two-thirds full. Bake 20 minutes until risen, and serve.

Double Choc-Chip Cookies

These cookies are the ultimate chocolate experience—double the chocolate, double the taste!

MAKES 14

⅔ cup butter
⅔ cup sugar
1 egg
1–2 tsp vanilla extract
1¾ cups all-purpose flour
1 tsp baking powder
2oz good-quality semisweet
  chocolate, broken into pieces
2oz good-quality white chocolate,
  broken into pieces

1 Preheat the oven to 350°F. Lightly grease a baking sheet.

2 Beat together the butter and sugar until pale and fluffy. Beat in the egg and vanilla extract. Sift the flour and baking powder together and beat into the mixture. Add the chocolate and stir until mixed.

3 Place 5–6 rounded tbsp of the cookie mixture onto the baking sheet at a time, leaving plenty of space between them as the cookies will almost double in size. Bake 12–15 minutes until golden. Let cool on the baking sheet, 2–3 minutes, then transfer to a wire rack to cool completely. Cookies can be stored in an airtight container for up to 5 days.

Brandy Snaps
with passion fruit mascarpone

These lacy ginger cookies are curled around the handle of a wooden spoon. They turn crisp as they cool and taste wonderful with a creamy mascarpone and passion fruit filling.

SERVES 4–6

4 tbsp butter, melted, plus extra
  for greasing
1 cup all-purpose flour
1 tsp ground ginger
1–2 tsp ground allspice (optional)
4 tbsp sugar
2 tbsp light corn syrup
1 tsp grated lemon peel
1 tbsp lemon juice
Filling
1 cup mascarpone cheese
2 passion fruits, halved
2 tbsp confectioners' sugar
⅔ cup heavy cream

1 Preheat the oven to 350°F. Grease two baking sheets and the handle of a wooden spoon with butter.

2 Sift the flour with the ground ginger. Add the allspice, if using. Melt the butter with the sugar and syrup in a saucepan over low heat. Remove from the heat and gradually stir in the flour mixture, then add the lemon peel and juice. Beat the mixture vigorously until it is thoroughly combined, with no lumps remaining.

3 Unless you have a team of willing helpers, bake the brandy snaps in small batches, so that you can roll the hot cookies before they cool. Drop teaspoons of the mixture on one of the baking sheets, leaving plenty of room, at least 3in, for spreading. Bake 6–8 minutes until they have spread and turned a rich, golden brown.

4 Remove the baking sheet from the oven and place it on top of a food warmer. Immediately place the handle of the wooden spoon on the end of one of the brandy snaps. Use a flat-bladed knife to flip the cookie over the spoon handle, then quickly roll round the handle to make a tube. Ease the brandy snap off the handle and quickly repeat the process with the remaining cookies. If they become too brittle to roll, warm them in the oven until they become pliable again.

5 Make more batches of brandy snaps in the same way, using the baking sheets alternately and greasing them each time. While the last batch is baking, make the filling. Put the mascarpone in a bowl. Scoop the passion fruit pulp into the bowl. Beat in the confectioners' sugar.

6 In a separate bowl, whip the cream to soft peaks, then fold into the mascarpone mixture. Fit a pastry bag with a plain tip and fill with the mixture. Pipe a little into either end of each brandy snap. Don't attempt to fill the brandy snaps completely. Serve at once.

Cook's Tip

Don't fill the brandy snaps too far ahead of serving or they will turn soggy.

Spiced Palmiers
with apples & raisins

These little cookies are delightfully tasty when served with this tangy apple compote and fresh cream.

MAKES 36

1½lb ready-made puff pastry
4 tbsp sugar
2 tbsp confectioners' sugar
1 tsp ground cinnamon, plus extra,
   for dusting
1–2 tsp ground ginger
1–2 tsp grated nutmeg
⅔ cup heavy cream, lightly whipped,
   to serve
Compote
1lb tart dessert apples, peeled,
   cored, and coarsely chopped
4 tbsp sugar
1 tbsp raisins
1 tbsp dried cherries or cranberries
2 tsp grated orange peel

1 Roll out the pastry thinly and trim to a 10 x 16in rectangle. Halve the pastry to make two smaller rectangles. Sift the sugar, confectioners' sugar, cinnamon, ginger, and nutmeg together. Dust both sides of each pastry sheet with about a quarter of the spiced sugar.

2 Working one rectangle at a time, lay the pastry on a floured work surface with the longest edge nearest you. Fold the pastry in half, away from you, then unfold to give a crease down the middle. Fold the edge of the pastry nearest you halfway to the crease and repeat with the edge of the pastry furthest away. Dust liberally with more of the spiced sugar.

3 Repeat the fold so that the edge nearest you meets the edge furthest away in the middle where you creased the pastry originally. Dust again with sugar. Reserve any leftover sugar.

4 Finally, fold again down the crease to give a long, thin rectangle. This will mean that you have six layers in all. Repeat the process with the second rectangle. Wrap each one in plastic wrap and put in the freezer to rest, 1 hour.

5 Preheat the oven to 350°F. Remove the pastry from the freezer and dust with any remaining spiced sugar. Using a sharp knife, cut each piece crosswise into eighteen slices. Lay the slices well spaced apart on a baking sheet. Bake 10 minutes, then turn and bake until golden, 5–10 minutes. Cool on a wire rack.

6 Meanwhile, put all the ingredients for the apple compote into a saucepan. Cover and cook over a gentle heat until the apple has softened, about 15 minutes. Stir well and set aside to cool.

7 Serve the spiced palmiers topped with the apple compote and whipped cream and dusted with ground cinnamon.

5

Crème de la Crème
Drop-dead gorgeous frozen desserts

Sweethearts

Take aim with Cupid's bow and discover the surest way to seduce your significant other with these passionate delights!

MAKES 2

4oz good-quality white chocolate,
  broken into pieces
1 tbsp light corn syrup
1 tbsp brandy
⅔ cup heavy cream
2 fresh strawberries, to serve
Strawberry sauce
1 cup strawberries, hulled
1 tbsp confectioners' sugar, plus extra
  for dusting

1 Place the chocolate in a heatproof bowl. Add the syrup and brandy. Place the bowl over a pan of gently simmering water and melt the chocolate, stirring the mixture occasionally.

2 Remove from the heat and let cool slightly. Whip the cream to soft peaks and carefully fold it into the chocolate mixture. Spoon into two ½ cup heart-shaped molds and let set in the refrigerator, at least 2 hours.

3 To make the sauce, blend the strawberries in a food processor with the confectioners' sugar. Press through a strainer to remove the seeds.

4 Run a knife gently around the edge of each chocolate heart, then carefully invert the molds and transfer onto two dessert plates. Drizzle the sauce around the hearts and decorate with the fresh strawberries. Dust with extra confectioners' sugar.

Blue Lagoon Ice Cream

If you want to make plain vanilla ice cream, omit the blueberry sauce and meringues, and freeze. Or, if you want to use any other fruit or chocolate sauce, swirl them in, as for the blueberries, at the end.

SERVES 6

⅔ cup milk
½ vanilla bean
2 egg yolks
5 tbsp sugar
2 cups blueberries
1 tbsp water
1 tbsp white rum
1 cup heavy cream
1½oz store-bought meringues

1 Put the milk and vanilla bean in a saucepan and bring to almost boiling over low heat. Take off the heat and remove the vanilla bean. Whisk the egg yolks and 4 tbsp of the sugar with a hand-held electric mixer until pale and slightly thickened, then lightly whisk in the milk.

2 Return to a clean heavy-based, nonstick saucepan. Cook over low heat, stirring continuously, until the mixture thickens to the consistency of heavy cream and coats the back of a spoon. Cover with plastic wrap and let cool. Meanwhile, cook the blueberries with the rest of the sugar and the water for 2 minutes until softened. Let cool, then stir in the rum.

3 Whip the cream until it forms stiff peaks and fold into the cold custard. Pour into a shallow freezerproof container and freeze until half-frozen, about 2–3 hours, then beat with a hand-held electric mixer to break down any ice crystals. Repeat this process at least twice more until the ice cream holds its shape. Alternatively, churn in an ice cream maker.

4 Swirl the meringues through the ice cream, followed quickly by the blueberry sauce, to make a marbled pattern. Spoon into a clean freezerproof container and freeze until firm. Remove from the freezer 20–30 minutes before serving.

Fig & Armagnac Ice Cream

The more ripe and flavorful the figs that you use, the better this sophisticated ice cream will taste.

SERVES 4–6

1lb ripe fresh figs, cut into quarters
3 tbsp Armagnac or sherry
4 egg yolks
¾ cup sugar
1¼ cups milk
1¼ cups heavy cream
1 tsp vanilla extract
Fresh figs cut in slices, to serve

1 Put the figs in a food processor with the Armagnac or sherry and process to a puree. Meanwhile, heat the milk to almost boiling in a saucepan over low heat.

2 Whisk the egg yolks with ½ cup of the sugar with a hand-held electric mixer until pale and slightly thickened, then lightly whisk in the hot milk.

3 Return to a clean, nonstick saucepan. Cook over low heat, stirring continuously, until the mixture thickens to the consistency of heavy cream and coats the back of a spoon. Cover with plastic wrap and let cool.

4 Lightly whip the cream until it forms soft peaks, then fold it into the cold custard with the pureed figs and vanilla extract. Taste the mixture and add the remaining sugar, if needed.

5 Pour into a shallow freezerproof container and freeze until half-frozen, about 2–3 hours, then beat with a hand-held electric mixer to break down any ice crystals. Repeat this process at least twice more until the ice cream holds its shape. Alternatively, churn in an ice cream maker.

6 Remove from the freezer 20–30 minutes before serving. Serve in scoops with slices of fresh figs.

Marshmallow & Chocolate Ice Cream

This rich, luxurious ice cream is even more indulgent when drizzled with a rich chocolate sauce.

SERVES 8

9oz sweet chocolate, broken
  into pieces
7oz marshmallows
3 tbsp water
2 x 14oz cartons fresh custard sauce
1¼ cups heavy cream

1 Place the chocolate in a heatproof bowl with three-quarters of the marshmallows. Add the water and set the bowl over a saucepan of gently simmering water. Melt the chocolate and stir until smooth, then let cool a little.

2 Stir the cooled chocolate mixture into the custard sauce. Chop the remaining marshmallows and fold into the mixture. Lightly whip the cream and fold in. Pour the mixture into a 5 cup terrine or loaf pan and freeze until hard. You may want to line the bottom of the pan with waxed paper to make it easier to unmold.

3 To serve, dip the base of the mold in hot water and invert on a serving plate. Cut the ice cream into thick slices.

White Chocolate Parfait

This heavenly little dessert may look innocent enough, but it will appeal to your most devilish instincts!

SERVES 4

6oz good-quality white chocolate,
  broken into pieces
2 tbsp milk
1 vanilla bean
4 egg yolks
¾ cup confectioners' sugar
1¼ cups heavy cream

1 Melt the chocolate with the milk in a heatproof bowl set over a pan of simmering water. Let cool.

2 Split the vanilla bean lengthwise and scrape out the seeds. Mix the seeds with the egg yolks and the confectioners' sugar, then whisk with a hand-held electric mixer until light and fluffy. Stir in the melted chocolate.

3 Lightly whip the cream and fold into the mixture. Divide the mousse between four custard cups, ramekins, or dariole molds, and freeze for a minimum of 4 hours until firm.

4 To serve, briefly dip the base of the molds into warm water and invert on serving plates.

Candied Fruit Bombe

You can make this classic dessert weeks in advance, so it's great for entertaining. As a short-cut, you could use a good-quality ready-made vanilla pudding instead of the egg custard in the recipe.

SERVES 6

4 tbsp dark rum or brandy
1 cup mixed dried fruit, such as apricots, raisins, figs, cherries, and cranberries, chopped
1 cup milk
1 vanilla bean
2 egg yolks
4 tbsp sugar
1 cup heavy cream
2oz good-quality semisweet chocolate, grated
Fresh figs, to serve
Fresh mint sprigs, to decorate

1 Pour the rum or brandy over the fruit and soak overnight. The next day, heat the milk and vanilla bean to simmering point in a saucepan over low heat. Take off the heat and remove the vanilla bean. Whisk the egg yolks and sugar with a hand-held electric mixer until pale and slightly thickened, then whisk in the hot milk.

2 Return to a clean heavy-based, nonstick saucepan. Cook over low heat, stirring continuously with a wooden spoon until the mixture thickens to the consistency of heavy cream and coats the back of a spoon. Cover with plastic wrap and let cool.

3 Lightly whip the cream until it forms soft peaks, then fold it into the cold custard. Freeze in a shallow freezerproof container until half-frozen, about 2–3 hours, then whisk to break down any ice crystals and return to the freezer. Repeat this process at least twice more until the ice cream holds its shape. Alternatively, churn in an ice cream maker. Mix in the rum-soaked fruits and the chocolate.

4 Spoon into a plastic wrap-lined 2lb pudding basin or six individual pudding basins. Freeze until firm. Remove from the freezer 30 minutes before serving. Turn out and remove the plastic wrap. Serve with fresh figs and decorate with mint sprigs.

Persimmon & Passion Fruit Ice Cream

This dessert has a beautiful pale primrose color and refreshing taste. Allow the ice cream to thaw slightly or "ripen" before serving to let the full flavor develop.

SERVES 4

3 ripe persimmons
3 passion fruits, halved
Juice of 1 lemon
5 tbsp sugar
1¼ cups heavy cream
Extra passion fruit pulp, to serve

1 Cut the top off each persimmon and spoon the persimmon flesh into a bowl, using a teaspoon to scrape as much flesh off the skins as possible. Place a strainer over the bowl. Scrape the passion fruit pulp into the strainer, then press it through with the back of a spoon, leaving the black seeds behind.

2 Spoon the mixture into a food processor, add the lemon juice and sugar and process to a fine puree. With the motor running, gradually add the cream until well combined.

3 Pour into a freezerproof container and freeze until half-frozen, about 2–3 hours, then beat to break up any ice crystals. Repeat this process twice more until the ice cream holds its shape. Alternatively, churn in an ice cream maker.

4 Before serving, let the ice cream soften for 20–30 minutes. Serve in scoops with a little passion fruit pulp spooned over the top.

Fresh Orange Ice Cream Cake

This refreshingly fruity ice cream cake is the perfect dessert to cool you down after a sizzling summer barbeque!

SERVES 8

4 oranges
5 eggs, separated
1¼ cups sugar
2 cups heavy cream
4oz ladyfingers
5 tbsp Grand Marnier

1 Line a 9in springform cake pan with plastic wrap.

2 Carefully cut the peel off one orange, removing as much of the white pith as possible. Cut between the separating membranes and lift out the segments. Arrange around the base of the cake pan.

3 Grate the peel of the remaining three oranges and set aside. Squeeze the juice into a saucepan. Bring to a boil and cook until reduced by half.

4 Place the egg yolks in a large bowl with 1 cup of the sugar and beat with a hand-held electric mixer until thick and frothy. Whisk in the reduced orange juice and grated peel and let cool. Lightly whip the cream until it has the same consistency as the custard, then fold into the orange custard.

5 Whisk the egg whites to stiff peaks and whisk in the remaining sugar, a tablespoon at a time. Next, fold the mixture into the orange cream.

6 Pour half the mixture over the orange segments in the cake pan. Dip the ladyfingers into the Grand Marnier and arrange in a layer across the orange cream. Spoon the remaining mixture over, cover, and freeze for 7–8 hours.

7 Invert the frozen orange cake onto a serving plate and place in the refrigerator for 30 minutes before serving.

Chocolate & Brandy Truffles

These rich and creamy dark chocolate-centered truffles are flavored with real brandy and coated with cocoa powder. They're perfect at the end of a meal, and make an impressive gift when wrapped.

MAKES 20–30

8oz good-quality semisweet chocolate, broken into pieces
1 tbsp brandy
1¼ cups heavy cream
1oz butter, cut into cubes
Unsweetened cocoa powder, for coating
Confectioners' sugar, for dusting

1 Place the chocolate in a bowl with the brandy.

2 Heat the cream in a pan and bring to a boil. Pour over the chocolate, stirring until the mixture is smooth and glossy and the chocolate pieces have melted. Add the cubes of butter, a few at a time, beating until they melt in. Place in the refrigerator until the mixture is on the point of setting.

3 Beat the mixture with a hand-held electric mixer until light and fluffy, 3–4 minutes. Return to the refrigerator to set completely.

4 Scoop out teaspoons of the truffle mixture, roll into balls, and coat in the cocoa powder. Dust with confectioner's sugar to serve.

Lychee Sorbet

Elderflower cordial adds a wonderful, scented flavor to this simple refreshing sorbet, but if it's hard to find, freshly made lemonade will give a similar end result. Whipped egg white is added to lighten the texture.

SERVES 6

6 tbsp sugar
1 cup water
14oz can pitted lychees in syrup
1 tbsp elderflower cordial
1 egg white

1 Heat the sugar and water in a saucepan over low heat until the sugar has dissolved. Bring to the boil and simmer for 1 minute. Remove from the heat and let cool.

2 Puree the lychees and their syrup in a food processor or blender, then pass through a strainer, pressing down well to extract all the juice. Add the elderflower cordial and the cooled sugar-water syrup.

3 Pour the mixture into a shallow freezerproof container and freeze until it just begins to hold its shape, about 2–3 hours.

4 Whisk the egg white until it forms soft peaks, then add it to the half-frozen sorbet mixture. Continue freezing and whisking by hand twice more until the mixture becomes thick and creamy. Freeze until required.

5 Remove the sorbet from the freezer and put in the refrigerator 5–10 minutes before serving.

Black Currant & White Rum Fool

A fool is a combination of pureed fruit, custard, and whipped cream—not unlike an unfrozen ice cream mixture. Tart fruit seem to work best, so rhubarb, gooseberries, plums, or, as here, black currants make a good choice.

SERVES 4

4 cups fresh or frozen black currants
½ cup sugar
2 tbsp fresh orange juice
2 tbsp white rum
½ cup milk
½ vanilla bean
2 egg yolks
1 cup heavy cream

1 Cook the black currants, half the sugar, and orange juice in a covered saucepan until very soft, about 5 minutes. Let cool. Puree in a food processor or blender. Push the juice and pulp through a strainer. Stir in the white rum and set aside.

2 For the custard, heat the milk and vanilla bean together in a saucepan over a low heat until almost boiling. Take off the heat and remove the vanilla bean. Whisk the egg yolks and the remaining sugar together until pale and slightly thickened, then whisk in the milk.

3 Return the mixture to a clean heavy-based, nonstick saucepan. Cook over a low heat, stirring continuously, until the mixture thickens to the consistency of heavy cream. Cover the surface with plastic wrap and let cool.

4 Whip the cream to soft peaks. Stir the black currant puree into the custard, then gently fold in the whipped cream. Stir gently until it thickens slightly, then spoon into glasses and chill before serving.

Exotic Iced Delight

Indulge yourself in this voluptuously
creamy mango ice cream dessert. Serve
with pecan nuts and maple syrup.

SERVES 2–4

1 large mango, peeled and pitted
1¼ cups custard sauce (see tip) or
    carton fresh custard
1¼ cups heavy cream
Chopped toasted pecans and maple syrup,
    to decorate

1 Blend the mango flesh to a smooth
puree in a food processor. Pour the
custard sauce into a large bowl and stir in
the mango puree. Whip the cream until it
forms soft peaks and gently fold it into the
custard mixture.

2 Pour the mixture into a shallow
freezerproof container and cover with an
airtight lid. Freeze 1 hour, then beat with a
fork to break up any large ice crystals.

3 Return the ice cream to the freezer for
2 hours, then beat again. Finally, return to
the freezer for 4 hours, or until frozen.
Scoop the ice cream into glasses, sprinkle
with pecans, and drizzle with maple syrup
before serving.

Cook's Tip

To make the custard sauce: Mix 2 tsp
cornstarch with 2 tbsp light cream in a cup.
Beat 2 egg yolks in a bowl until pale, then
stir in the cornstarch mix. Heat 1 cup light
cream with ¼ cup sugar in a pan. When
hot, pour half the hot cream onto the egg
mixture, stirring constantly, then add the
mixture to the remaining hot cream in the
pan. Cook about 5 minutes, stirring
constantly, until thickened, then stir in
½ tsp vanilla extract. Cover and let cool.

Mandarin Paradise Parfait

Simple to make yet spectacular to look at, this is the ideal kids' party treat.

SERVES 4

11oz canned mandarin oranges,
  drained and juice reserved
3oz package Jell-O orange-flavored
  gelatin dessert
6oz cream cheese
Whipped cream, to decorate
Fresh citrus and passion fruits, to decorate

1 Add boiling water to the mandarin juice to make 1½ cups of liquid and dissolve the Jell-O in it. Hand-beat the cream cheese until smooth and creamy. Add ½ cup of the Jell-O mixture, beating thoroughly to avoid lumps.

2 Cut the mandarins up coarsely and add to the cream cheese mixture. Pour half of the remaining Jell-O mixture into four tall parfait glasses and place in the coldest part of the refrigerator to set, 3–4 hours.

3 When ready, pour half the soft cheese mixture into the parfait glasses on top of the set Jell-O and set, as above. Repeat the two layers again and set well. Decorate with whipped cream.

4 Peel and chop a selection of citrus fruits, such as oranges, grapefruit, and clementines. Squeeze the juice and seeds of one or two passion fruits over them. Use to garnish the parfaits, or serve in a separate bowl for a refreshing and colorful fruit salad accompaniment.

Variation

Instead of cream cheese, you can use a 5½oz can of evaporated milk. Other fruits and Jell-O flavors can be substituted as well, such as cherry jelly partnered with fresh cherries and grapes, or raspberry jelly with a berry fruit salad consisting of raspberries, blackberries, and blueberries.

Table of Equivalents

The following conversions and equivalents will provide useful guidelines for international readers to follow. There's just one golden rule to remember when you're preparing your ingredients: always stay with one system of measurement—that way you'll achieve the best results from these recipes.

Liquid Measures

½ tsp	=	2.5ml
1 tsp	=	5ml
2 tsp	=	10ml
1 tbsp	=	15ml
¼ cup	=	60ml
⅓ cup	=	75ml
½ cup	=	125ml
⅔ cup	=	150ml
¾ cup	=	185ml
1 cup	=	250ml
1¼ cups	=	300ml
1½ cups	=	375ml
1⅔ cups	=	400ml
1¾ cups	=	450ml
2 cups	=	500ml
2½ cups	=	600ml
3 cups	=	750ml
3½ cups	=	800ml
4 cups	=	1 liter
5 cups	=	1.2 liters
6 cups	=	1.5 liters
8 cups	=	2 liters

Dry Measures

¼oz	=	10g
½oz	=	15g
¾oz	=	20g
1oz	=	25g
1½oz	=	40g
2oz	=	50g
2½oz	=	65g
3oz	=	75g
3½oz	=	90g
4oz	=	115g
4½oz	=	130g
5oz	=	150g
5½oz	=	165g
6oz	=	175g
6½oz	=	185g
7oz	=	200g
8oz	=	225g
9oz	=	250g
10oz	=	275g
11oz	=	300g
12oz	=	350g
14oz	=	400g
15oz	=	425g
1lb	=	450g
1¼lb	=	500g
1½lb	=	675g
2lb	=	900g
2¼lb	=	1kg
3–3½lb	=	1.5kg
4–4½lb	=	1.75kg
5–5¼lb	=	2.25kg
6lb	=	2.75kg

Butter

1 tbsp	=	15g
2 tbsp	=	25g
3 tbsp	=	45g
4 tbsp	=	55g
5 tbsp	=	75g
6 tbsp	=	90g
⅓ cup	=	75g
½ cup	=	120g
⅔ cup	=	150g
¾ cup	=	175g
1 cup	=	225g
1½ cups	=	350g

Sugar

¼ cup	=	4 tbsp
⅓ cup	=	75g
scant ½ cup	=	100g
½ cup	=	120g
¾ cup	=	175g
scant 1 cup	=	200g
1 cup	=	225g
1¼ cups	=	275g

1½ cups	=	350g
1¾ cups	=	400g
2 cups	=	450g

Flour

¼ cup	=	25g
½ cup	=	55g
⅔ cup	=	75g
¾ cup	=	100g
1 cup	=	120g
1¼ cups	=	145g
1½ cups	=	175g
1¾ cups	=	200g
2 cups	=	225g
2¼ cups	=	250g
2½ cups	=	275g
3 cups	=	350g
3½ cups	=	400g
4 cups	=	450g
4¼ cups	=	500g
6½ cups	=	750g

Oven Temperatures

°F	°C	Gas
250	120	1
300	150	2
325	160	3
350	180	4
375	190	5
400	200	6
425	220	7
450	230	8
475	240	9
500	250	10

American culinary terms and their British equivalents

all-purpose flour	plain flour
baking soda	bicarbonate of soda
broiler	grill
confectioners' sugar	icing sugar
cornstarch	cornflour
cream puff paste	choux pastry
half-and-half cream	half-fat cream
heavy cream	double cream
jelly	jam
jelly roll	Swiss roll
ladyfingers	sponge fingers
light corn syrup	golden syrup
light cream	single cream
pan	tin
pastry bag	piping bag
persimmon	sharon fruit
pie shell	pastry case
preserved ginger	stem ginger
self-rising flour	self-raising flour
semisweet chocolate	plain chocolate
skillet	frying pan
sweet chocolate	milk chocolate
tart pan	flan tin
unsweetened chocolate	bitter plain chocolate
waxed paper	baking parchment

Index